Backyard **Bugs** & Creepy Crawlies

Scorpions

Ashley Lee

Explore other books at:
WWW.ENGAGEBOOKS.COM

VANCOUVER, B.C.

e → WWW.ENGAGEBOOKS.COM

Scorpions: Level 1
Backyard Bugs & Creepy Crawlies
Lee, Ashley 1995 –

Text © 2022 Engage Books
Design © 2022 Engage Books

Edited by: A.R. Roumanis

Text set in Epilogue

FIRST EDITION / FIRST PRINTING

LIBRARY AND ARCHIVES CANADA CATALOGUING IN PUBLICATION

Title: Scorpions / Ashley Lee.
Names: Lee, Ashley, author.
Description: Series statement: Backyard bugs & creepy-crawlies
Engaging readers: level 1, beginner.

Identifiers: Canadiana (print) 20250448542 | Canadiana (ebook) 20250448569
ISBN 978-1-77878-709-6 (hardcover)
ISBN 978-1-77878-718-1 (softcover)

Subjects:
LCSH: Scoripions—Juvenile literature.

Classification: LCC QL737.P94 C38 2025 | DDC J599.885—DC23

This project has been made possible in part by the Government of Canada.

Canada

Contents

What Are Scorpions?

Scorpions are arachnids (ah-rack-nids). They are related to spiders.

4

Scorpions were one of the first animals to start living on land. Land scorpions are about 420 million years old.

What Do Scorpions Look Like?

Scorpions have hard shells. They protect their soft bodies.

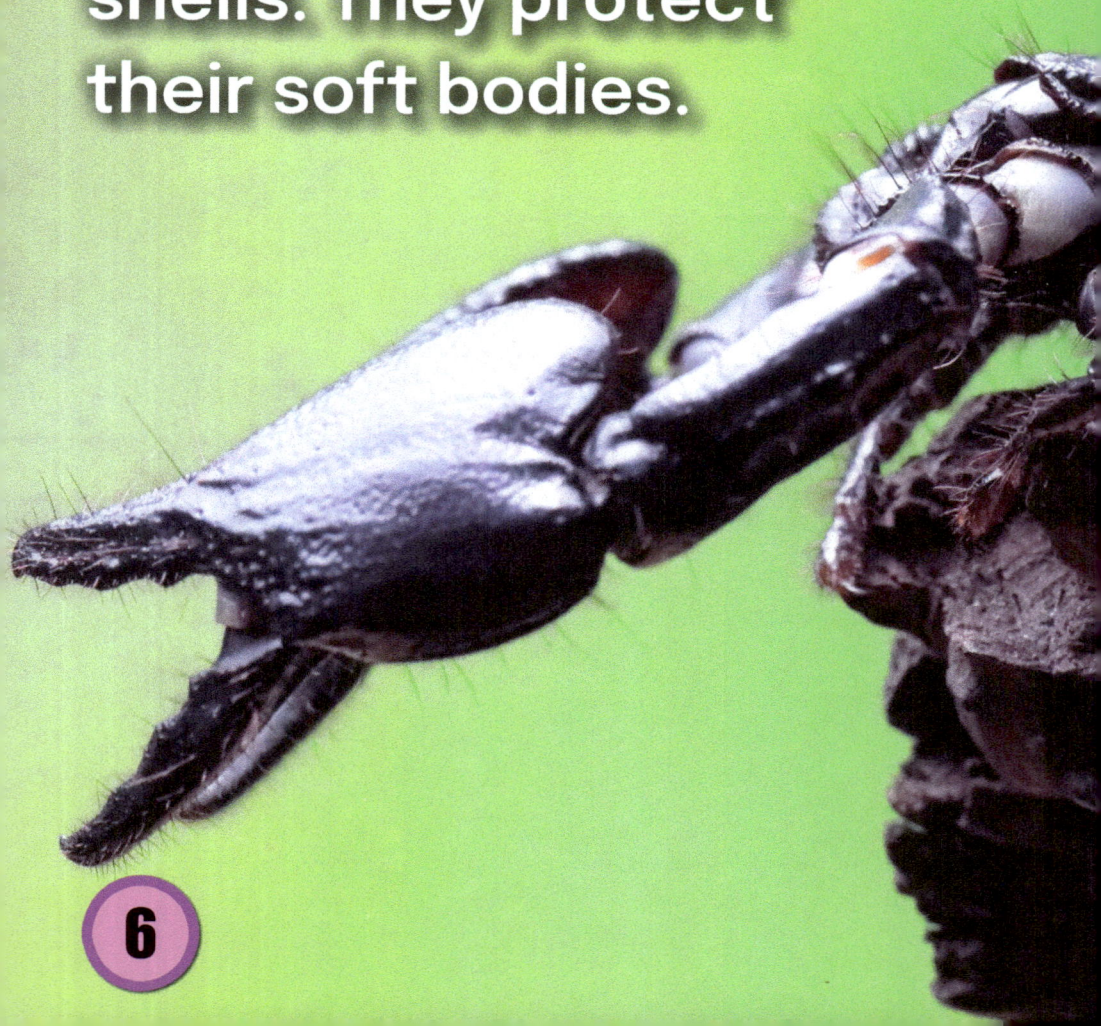

Scorpions have a stinger at the end of their bodies. It has **venom** in it.

Key Word

Venom: the poison made by some animals.

Scorpions have two sharp pincers. They use them to grab food.

Scorpions can have up to 12 eyes. But they cannot see very well.

Where Do Scorpions Live?

Scorpions live all over the world. Some scorpions live in deserts. Others live in forests or grasslands.

Some scorpions dig holes to live in. These are called burrows.

11

What Do Scorpions Eat?

Scorpions eat any small animal they can catch. They often eat spiders or bugs.

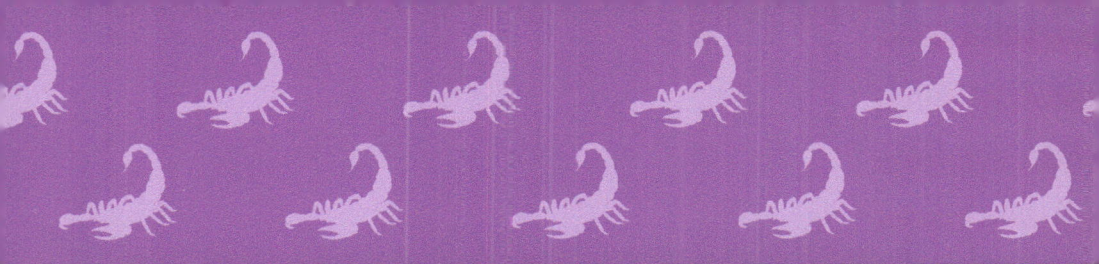

Some scorpions will eat small animals like lizards. Some will even eat other scorpions.

13

Some scorpions look for **prey**. Many do not. They sit and wait until an animal is nearby.

Key Word

Prey: an animal that is hunted and eaten by another animal.

They then run up and grab it. They will sting it if it is big or fights back.

15

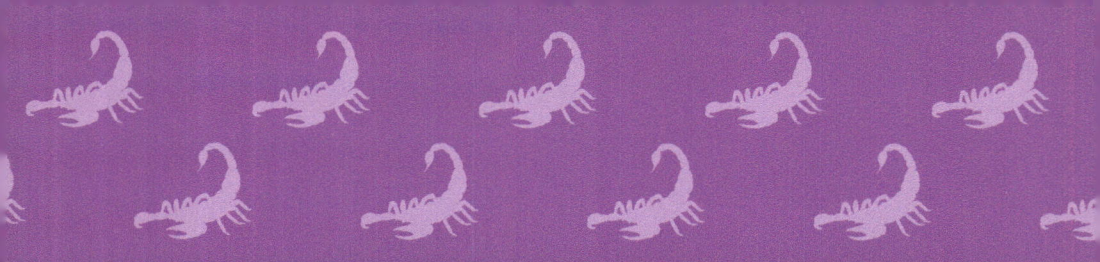

Scorpion Behavior

Scorpions often hide during the day. They hide in their burrows or under rocks.

Scorpions are more active at night. They may do this to get away from other animals that want to eat them.

Most scorpions live alone. They are only around others when they are born or during **mating**.

Key Word

Mating: making babies.

A few scorpions live in groups. They help each other catch food.

Scorpion Life Cycle

Scorpions do not lay eggs. They give birth to babies.

Baby scorpions are often white. They ride on their mother's back.

Young scorpions stay with their mom for up to two years. Some scorpion moms might eat them if they stay too long.

Most scorpions live
for three to eight
years. Some can live
as long as 25 years.

23

Fun Facts

Scorpions can go a whole year without eating.

Some scorpions dance before mating.

Some scorpions make noise by rubbing their legs together.

Scorpions glow under a special light called UV light.

Are Scorpions Helpful or Harmful?

A few kinds of scorpions are dangerous to humans. Their sting can kill.

But they may also be helpful. Scientists are studying scorpion venom to see if it can be made into medicine.

Are Scorpions in Danger?

Some scorpions are not in danger. But many scorpions are in danger of dying out.

One problem is that people are taking wild scorpions home. They are keeping them as pets.

Quiz

Test your knowledge of scorpions by answering the following questions. The questions are based on what you have read in this book. The answers are listed on the bottom of the next page.

1 Are scorpions related to spiders?

2 Can scorpions see well?

3 Do some scorpions dig holes to live in?

4 Do most scorpions live alone?

5 Do scorpions lay eggs?

6 Can scorpions go a whole year without eating?

Explore other books in the
Backyard Bugs & Creepy Crawlies series!

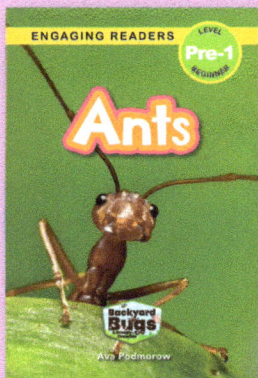

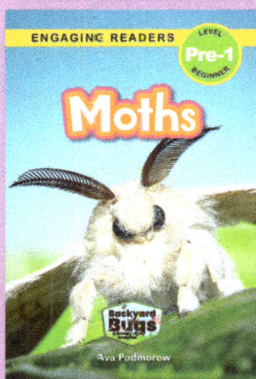

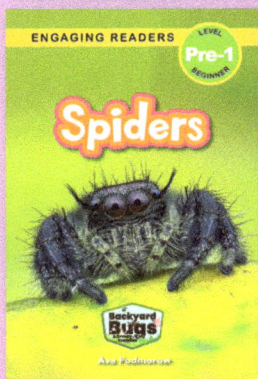

ENGAGING READERS · LEVEL Pre-1 BEGINNER
Ants
Backyard Bugs
Ava Podmorow

ENGAGING READERS · LEVEL Pre-1 BEGINNER
Beetles
Backyard Bugs
Victoria Hazlehurst

ENGAGING READERS · LEVEL Pre-1 BEGINNER
Caterpillars
Backyard Bugs
Ava Podmorow

ENGAGING READERS · LEVEL Pre-1 BEGINNER
Grasshoppers
Backyard Bugs
Ava Podmorow

ENGAGING READERS · LEVEL Pre-1 BEGINNER
Moths
Backyard Bugs
Ava Podmorow

ENGAGING READERS · LEVEL Pre-1 BEGINNER
Snails
Backyard Bugs
Ava Podmorow

ENGAGING READERS · LEVEL Pre-1 BEGINNER
Spiders
Backyard Bugs
Ava Podmorow

ENGAGING READERS · LEVEL Pre-1 BEGINNER
Wasps
Backyard Bugs
Sarah Harvey

ENGAGING READERS · LEVEL Pre-1 BEGINNER
Worms
Backyard Bugs
Victoria Hazlehurst

Visit www.engagebooks.com to explore more Engaging Readers.

Answers: 1. Yes 2. No 3. Yes 4. Yes 5. No 6. Yes